"How to" Market Your Book

You have written your book, and now what?

- Step #1: Get the book published; and
- Step #2: Marketing, Marketing, and more Marketing!

If you thought writing and publishing was the hardest part of being an author, you would be wrong … Marketing is by far the hardest, most time consuming, AND THE MOST IMPORTANT!

It is time for you to:

And, Your Book is Your Product!

- AND -

Marketing Your Book is an on-going Process …one that should start with Creating a Book Marketing Plan. This book includes a Book Marketing Plan Template to get you started.

"How to" Market Your Book

Including a Book Marketing Plan Template

Mary D. Scott, PMP

THIS BOOK IS PUBLISHED BY MARY D. SCOTT, PMP

Book Cover is designed by Mary D. Scott, PMP

www.spiritdrivenevents.com

Library of Congress Cataloging-in-Publication Data available upon request.
ISBN 978-1463761813
ISBN 1463761813

Printed in the United States of America

June 2011

†

Books by Mary D. Scott
Spirit Driven Events – Fascinating and Enlightening True Stories

Dedication

This book is dedicated to all my fellow authors, family, and friends who have supported my writing, editing, and publishing of this book
- **Mary D. Scott, PMP**

Reviews

"You have covered appropriately, an audience full of query, by producing a book that answers marketing and distribution loop holes in such a few short pages that it is amazing. But you also prioritized many pertinent concepts in an understandable format. Nicely accomplished."
- **Dr. Judith A. Holton**

"Well done. The book is concise and easy to follow."
- **Deborah L. Weltin, Author**

"There are many self-help marketing books available today but none explain book marketing more concise and completely than Mary D. Scott's book. **"How to" Market Your Book** is a valuable tool that will keep you away from the pitfalls of trial and error and on the path to having a best seller."
- **Mary Ruth Hughes, Author**
WillowVistaBooks.com

"Mary Scott has compiled and written an excellent road map to help you through the marketing-promotions maze. A no-fluff, no nonsense, action-item-driven plan with your success in mind!"
- **Madeline (M.M.) Gornell - Author**
www.mmgornell.com

"Mary Scott has come up with a template and directions for those who hate the work of creating an essential marketing plan to help make their book a business success. This could be useful for those right-brained writers who might be tempted to skip that part."
- **Bob Isbill, President High Desert Branch of the California Writers Club**

Reviews

"Mary has taken an intimidating area of business for any author and organized it into concise, easy to understand steps. A great tool for the up-and-coming writer."
- Roberta Smith, Author
BertaBooks.com

"As an author, switching from the art of writing the book to the business of marketing it is a stressful challenge. Mary provides a template that is incredibly simple to use which makes you think, organizes your marketing plan, and saves time on your goal to making your book available in a most effective way. Finally someone makes it so much easier!"-
F.L. Gold, PhD, MFT, CTACC
http://freddiesblog.typepad.com

"Writing a book is like giving birth. Marketing a book is like raising a child. Both tasks are painful, yet the potential for joy and fulfillment is endless. Just ask any parent or successful author. Mary Scott accomplishes the impossible. She brings simplicity to the overwhelming task of marketing a book. Introvert and extrovert alike will discover the road to success. **"How to" Market Your Book** is a MUST read for every author."
- Denny Stanz, Author
www.DennyStanz.com

"In **"How To" Market your Book**, Mary Scott gives readers the ultimate marketing tool: a personal template to guide an author through all the steps to success. Clear, concise, and easy to follow, "How To" covers every aspect of marketing in the fast changing world of books and is the only guide an author will ever need."
- Anne Bancroft Fowler PhD, Author, Editor

Contents

PREFACE

I have written this book as an aide to other authors who struggle with the marketing of their book. Writing a book is hard enough, but getting published and doing all the marketing is really tough, time consuming, and expensive. Whether you self-publish or go the traditional publishing route, you will still have to market your book, and you will still need to have a Book Marketing Plan. The first step in marketing is to create a Book Marketing Plan or otherwise sometimes referred to as a Book Proposal.

My hope for you (the reader and fellow author) is to give you a jump-start on creating your own Book Marketing Plan. I do this by including an easy to use Book Marketing Plan Template.

Happy Marketing

-   Mary D. Scott, PMP

SECTION I – Book Publishing and Marketing in General

1. Traditional Publishing versus Self-Publishing

1.1 Traditional Publishing

Typical dream: You write a book and submit it to a publisher. You hope to sit back and get rich collecting royalties so you have time to write another book. Now, step into the real world! Generally, you will write and submit query letter after query letter to numerous traditional publishers and will receive numerous rejection letters (50 or more, unless you are very lucky and have an inside connection). Oh yes, and you most likely will also need a literary agent just to get your book manuscript in front of a traditional publisher. The first thing an agent will ask you is: *Do you have a Marketing Plan?* If not, they will tell you: *When you develop one, then come and see me.* This can go on for years and become nothing but a frustration for the author. Not to mention how hard it is to find a good literary agent. The frustration caused by the traditional publishing route is rapidly being replaced by Self-Publishing and Print on Demand companies, as well as, Electronic Publishing.

1.2 Self-Publishing and Electronic Publishing.

As authors get frustrated with the traditional publishing route, they start to research the self-publishing, print on demand, and electronic publishing routes. They find that even though they have to do most of the work, they are also in control of every aspect of how their book gets published (i.e. no demanding rewrites based on someone else's opinion; no quarrels over cover design, etc.) and they will receive the highest royalty because they cut out all of the frustrating middlemen. And the biggest plus is they do not have to write query letters and get rejections; and their book can be published in a much quicker time frame (maybe a month or so). Electronic Publishing is even quicker and easier to get your book out on the market.

2. Marketing

Whether you choose traditional, self-publish, or electronic publishing, a universal truth applies – YOU, THE AUTHOR – have sole responsibility to market your book. The marketing of your book should have started the day you started to write, but, unfortunately, most authors do not realize this and wait until after the book is written and published. If they chose the Traditional publishing route, they make the assumption they will get a book contract with a major publisher and that the publisher will handle all the marketing. This is not how it works. I will say it again, no matter what publishing route you choose, **you WILL have to do marketing for your book. So, let's talk Book Marketing Plan.**

SECTION II – Book Marketing Plan

3. Think Product and Think Process

There are TWO things I would like for you to keep in mind:

And, Your Book is Your Product!

- AND -

Marketing Your Book is an on-going Process …one that should start with Creating a Book Marketing Plan.

4. Components of a Book Marketing Plan

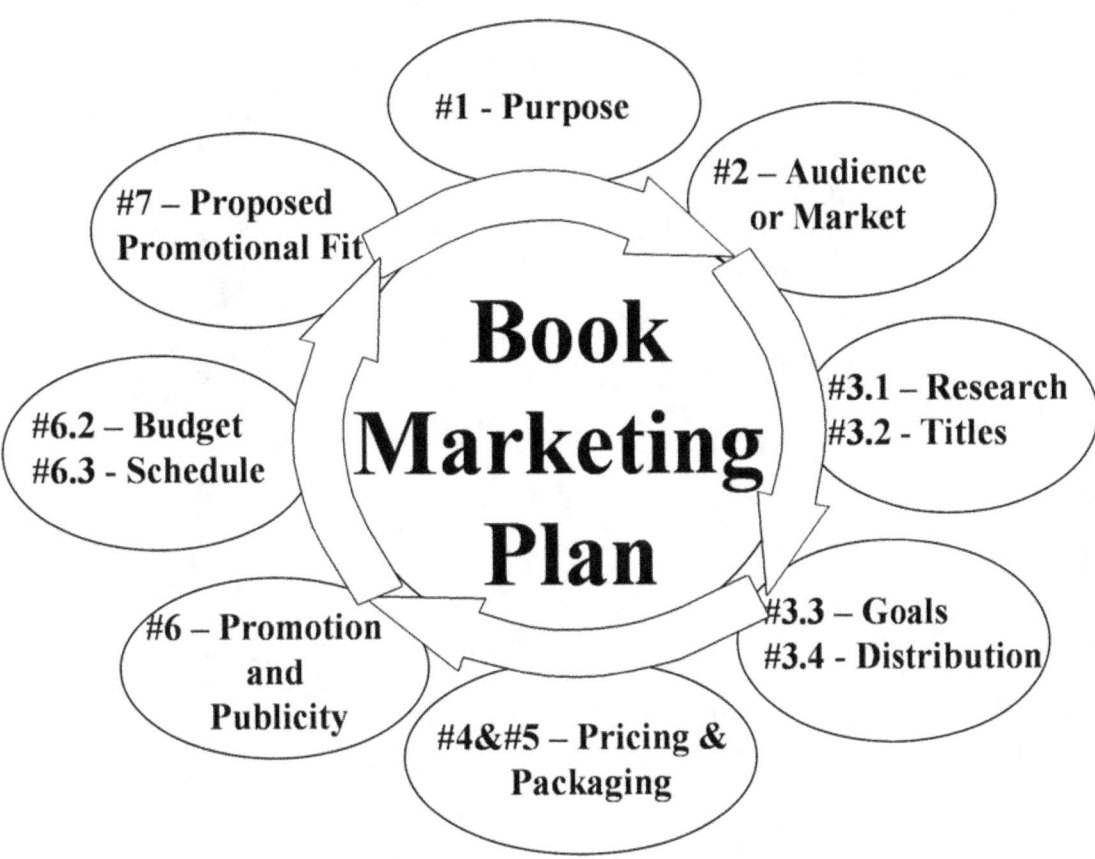

Eight major components of a Book Marketing Plan (BMP)

There are eight major components needed to properly create a Book Marketing Plan (BMP). Section #3 and #6 will notably be the largest of your completed BMP, as shown by the outline below:

1. **Purpose**
2. **Audience or Market**

3. **The Book**
   3.1 – Market Research
       3.1.1 – Strengths of my Book
       3.1.2 – Weaknesses of my Book
       3.1.3 – Opportunities for the success of my Book
       3.1.4 – Threats to the success of my Book
   3.2 – Competitive Titles
   3.3 – Marketing Goals
   3.4 – Distribution Channels

In the next section, I have included a "Book Marketing Plan Template" that contains built-in assistance within each segment of the BMP. The built-in assistance is in *italics*. You can re-create this template in your own Word processing program and complete your own Book Marketing Plan. Feel free to incorporate some of the ideas I provided in *italics*, into your BMP. If you would like the Microsoft Word version of this template, then visit www.spiritdrivenevents.com and send me an email request.

SECTION III – The Book Marketing Plan Template

Book Marketing Plan

For

Enter Title of Book Here

Version 1.0

Enter Date Here

Prepared for: *Publishing Company Name here*
[Street Address]
[City, State, Zip]

Prepared by: *Author's Name here, Author*
[Street Address]
[City, State, Zip]

Table of Contents

Book Marketing Plan
(Enter Book Title Here)

1. Purpose
In this section, describe the purpose for this document, for example:

This book marketing plan is a comprehensive overview of my potential book sales and promotional activities. The plan contains marketing strategies and activities, as well as, how I intend to position my book in the marketplace. It will also contain an analysis of my competition, strengths and weaknesses of my book, opportunities, and potential threats to the success of my book.

2. Audience or Market
In this section, provide "Who" the audience / market are for your book. Who did you write this book for? Think about what categories your book falls into, and then you can narrow your focus and target specific groups.

3. The Book
In this section, describe what kind of book this is. Check out who your competition is and list it here.

3.1 Market Research
In this section, describe all the market research you did and the results.

3.1.1 Strengths of my Book
In this section, based on your market research, describe the strengths of your book. How does your book stand out from your competitor's?

3.1.2 Weaknesses of my Book
In this section, based on your market research, describe the weaknesses of your book. Is your book just like your competitor's?

3.1.3 Opportunities for the success of my Book
In this section, based on your market research, describe the opportunities for your book.

3.1.4 Threats to the success of my Book
In this section, based on your market research, describe the Threats to the success of your book.

3.2 Competitive Titles

In this section, describe all the Competitive Titles you found during your market research.

3.3 Marketing Goals

Marketing is a full-time adventure. Make a Commitment and don't back away from it: Commitment: means to set up Goals: short term, intermediate, & long term Goals. In this section, describe your Marketing Goals, for example:

My goal for 2011 is to do 25 radio interviews and have 25 speaking engagements. My "big" goal is to have a company buy my book in bulk. My #1 target is Costco. Let's say they have 1000 stores. If they buy 100 books for each store, then 100 times 1000 = 100,000 books and, If I can earn $1.00 per book, that's $100,000.00 in income.

3.4 Distribution Channels

In this section, describe what Distribution Channels you are going to be using.

Choosing methods of distributions are a MUST for any successful marketing campaigns. Some methods of distribution are: Mass Market; Schools, Libraries, or Book Wholesalers such as: Baker, Taylor & Dunn or Ingram Distributing. Using Wholesalers = higher productivity & better market population/ less expensive & hits many.

4. Book Pricing

In this section, describe how you will price your book. Make sure you don't price it too high or too low. Research your competitor's pricing of their books.

5. Book Packaging

In this section, describe how you will design and package your book. This is your book's first impression so be creative and passionate when designing and packaging it.

6. Book Promotion and Publicity

In this section, describe how you will promote and publicize your book. How will you spread the word? What relationships will you build to help promote it?

6.1.1 Start Immediately

In this section, describe how you will immediately start to market your book.

You should begin the marketing of your book the day you start to write it. Your book will be stronger if you're committed to its success from the start. Let everyone know you are writing a book and what it is about. Ask your family, friends, and colleagues for feedback and advice.

6.1.2   Write a Press Release

In this section, describe how, when, where, and to whom you will send press releases. Include a sample of your press release in this section.

Write a press release and send it to the appropriate media and/or to any local newspaper in your area. If you are going to be attending an event and can get the Event Sponsor to do the press release, then that is even better.

6.1.2.1 Press Release Sample

In this section, include a sample of your press release.

Press Release Writing Tips:

Writing a press release is not difficult. Consider these tips to get you started:

- *Research how other authors wrote their press releases.*
- *Use either your own or your book publishing company's letterhead.*
- *Keep your focus on the most compelling aspects and/or relevant points of your book.*
- *Keep your press release brief (4 or 5 brief paragraphs). Choose your words wisely and use a combination of short and medium length sentences.*
- *Include the title of your book only once.*
- *Write about the book's topic and your angle for writing the book. Focus on the book's benefits for the reader.*
- *Write a compelling headline and keep it short (4 to 7 words).*
- *Write a short catchy sentence that ties directly with the headline, and will flow easily into the rest of the brief paragraph.*
- *Provide a link to your book's website where other information about you and your book may be found.*
- *Send your press release to editors of local newspapers in the cities where your Event will be held.*

6.1.3   Internet Marketing and Networking

Internet Marketing and Networking is a MUST. In this section, list all the places you are going to do your internet marketing and social networking. You can visit other websites related to your book's topic and get some ideas there. Make some comments on Blogs and leave a link back to your book's website.

- **<u>Facebook</u>**

    Facebook is a quick way to connect with many people. You can use Facebook Ads to market your book; you can create an Author Fan Club page; and you can announce your Events.

- **<u>Twitter</u>**

    Twitter is another social media avenue you can use, but, you need to establish a following before Twitter will be effective. www.twitter.com

- **<u>LinkedIn</u>**

    LinkedIn is a professional social networking website where you invite people to be LinkedIn to you. www.linkedin.com

- **<u>BLOG</u>**

    Create a BLOG and establish yourself as an expert among other Bloggers. Wordpress and Blogger.com are two places where you can set up your own BLOG.

- **<u>Podcasts</u>**

    Create Podcasts about your book; create an account with Podbean.com; and post your Podcasts for the public to listen to. In this section, list all of your Podcasts.

- **<u>YouTube</u>**

    Create 3-5 minute videos about your book and/or get yourself interviewed by answering ten frequently asked questions about your book's topic. You can post videos at www.youtube.com for free. In this section, list all of your YouTube videos.

- **<u>Webcasts</u>**

    Create webcasts about your book, and list them in this section.

- **<u>Book Daily Website</u>**

    The Book Daily website is a place to get you and your book showcased for free. This site will feature a chapter from your book and has thousands of potential viewers. www.bookdaily.com

- ## Internet Networking

  You can use Google to perform a search for online groups of authors and writers, and start networking online with them. There is a Poets and Writers website at www.pw.org. In this section, list your internet networking sites.

- ## Reporters Connection and Query

  Reporters Connection and Query - Join Reporter Connection for FREE and they will let you know, via email, when top journalists, and producers are doing stories on your subject. www.reporterconnection.com

- ## Sites/Bloggers

  Contact Book Bloggers and Reviewers to review your book, and list them in this section.

- ## Online Newsletters / Magazines / Website

  Contact online newsletters / Magazines / Websites and see if they will publish an article about you and your book or review your book, and list them in this section.

  Some places to start with are:
  - *Examiner.com.*
  - *Dan Poynter Online Newsletter*
  - *ChicGalleria.com*
  - *About.com*
  - *RickFrishman.com*
  - *At the following website http://www.wilsonweb.com you can download a free article called "The Six Simple Principles of Viral Marketing", by Dr. Ralph F. Wilson*

- ## Getting Corporate Sponsors

  Consider trying to obtain a grant from a Fortune 500 company in your industry to cover your book publicity and marketing expenses. Corporate Sponsors may be happy to do it because your book may educate their target market. In this section, list your potential Corporate Sponsors.

6.1.4   Build a Website for your Book

Creating a website for your book is a MUST. Get a domain name with the title of your book. If the domain name is not available, then add the word "book" at the end. Also register your book's title as a Blog. In this section, provide the details of the website you plan to build and what you plan to include on your website.

Items you should have on your website include the following:

- *Your photo and biography*
- *The book's cover and synopsis*
- *An Excerpt or Sample Chapter*
- *A press release*
- *A photo / video gallery, if applicable*
- *Your Schedule of Events*
- *Where to buy the book*
- *Readers Comments Section*
- *Link to your Blog*
- *Email address*
- *A Contact Us page*

Some places to get your domain name and/or to build your website:

- *www.1and1.com*
- *www.officelive.com*
- *Hostmaster*
- *GoDaddy.com*
- *Squarespace.com*

Other Website / Email Tips:

- *Send a freebie with every book purchased from your site, no matter how small, a book mark would be a good example.*
- *In your email signature line, include your book and website link*
- *Develop Search Engine Optimization (SEO) keywords for your website to draw traffic*
- *Create a video and post it on YouTube and on your website*
- *Link to other websites and ask for reciprocal links to your website*
- *Publish electronic newsletters or articles*

6.1.5   Give Your Book Away

Give your book away, but not just to media type people. Send a free copy to people who gave you advice. Have your book reviewed by other authors to try and create a buzz about it. Don't give away your books to anyone other than to people that can and will help you promote and market your books. And, make sure you get the person's okay before sending your book for review; otherwise you can end up wasting a lot of time and money. After you receive the reviews back, consider mentioning them on the acknowledgments page prior to printing. In this section, list the people to whom you gave your book.

6.1.6   Give Free Information and/or Promotional Items

Give away free information and/or promotional items that have your contact information and website address on it. List your items in this section.

Promotional Items:

- *Business cards - Vistaprint.com*
- *Book marks - create a colorful card with your book's cover, a brief description of the book, contact information, and your website address*
- *T-Shirts- print t-shirts with the book's title and/or cover on it - Vistaprint.com*
- *Car magnets- Vistaprint.com*
- *Ink pens- Vistaprint.com*
- *Key rings- Vistaprint.com*
- *Posters - Costco; Staples; and now Vistaprint offers poster printing*
- *Poster board displays - Staples*
- *Banners- Vistaprint.com*
- *Sample books*
- *Postcards – Vistaprint.com*

6.1.7   Public Speaking

Public speaking is a MUST to promote your book. Most people do not like public speaking, and if you are one of those people, then consider joining a local Toastmasters group. In this section, list all the clubs, groups, and organizations that might be interested in your topic.

Book Signings / Speaking

- *Libraries – Any and ALL*
- *Book stores – Any and ALL*
- *Look for writing clubs who might want to hear about your book*

- *Coffee shops*
- *Shopping malls – Any and All*
- *Conferences*
- *Soroptomist clubs*
- *Schools*
- *Book clubs*

\- **Arts / Crafts Festivals and Shows**

Search the internet for local and Other Arts /Crafts Festivals and Shows and list them in this section.

- *Local and Other Arts and Crafts Shows*
- *Local and Other Farmers Markets*

\- **Book Festivals**

Search the Internet for local and Other Book Festivals and list them in this section.

- *Local and other book festivals*
- *Pair yourself with another author to do events*
- *West Hollywood Park Book Faire*
- *San Luis Obispo Book Festival*
- *LA Times Book Festival*
- *Kern Festival of Writers*
- *Tucson Festival of Books*
- *Orange County Children's Book Festival*

\- **Networking**

In this section, list your Networking places.

- *Join local writers club. In California, there is the California Writers Club.*
- *Join a Chamber of Commerce and business networking groups*
- *Set-up events at clubs and other groups who might be interested in learning about your subject*
- *Public Safety Writers Assoc. (PSWA)*
- *Greater Los Angeles Writers Society (GLAWS)*

- <u>**Conferences**</u>

  In this section, list the Conferences you plan to attend.

  - *California Writers Club*
  - *Public Safety Writers Assoc. (PSWA)*
  - *Sisters in Crime*

- <u>**Conventions**</u>

  In this section, list the Conventions you plan to attend.

<u>**- Panels and Libraries**</u>

  In this section, list the Panels and Libraries where you plan to participate.

  - *HD CWC Author Panels*
  - *Book Fair / Festival Panels*
  - *Library panels*
  - *Conference panels*

- <u>**TV and Radio Shows**</u>

  In this section, list the TV and Radio Stations where you plan to participate.

6.1.8   Writing Contests / Awards

Check for Writing Contests and National Best Books Awards. Awards are not given away for free, you must enter a contest to get an award and they all charge a fee. In this section, list all the writing contests you plan to participate in.

Some ideas are:

- *California Writers Club*
- *2010 89th Edition Writer's Market: Listings of Contests and Awards, pgs. 1006 – 1070.*
- *Eric Hoffer*
- *Claymore Award*

6.1.9   Books to help Marketing Efforts

In this section, list all the books you plan to use to help your marketing efforts.

- ***2010 89th Edition Writer's Market:*** *This book includes the following in regards to Marketing:*
  - *Build a Platform (i.e Marketing) pgs. 71-75;*
  - *Creating Effective Press Releases, pgs. 76-77;*
  - *Listings of Consumer Magazines, pgs. 359 - 797;*
  - *Listings of Trade Journals, pgs. 798-962;*
  - *Listings of Newspapers, pgs. 963-971;*
  - *Listings of Contests and Awards, pgs. 1006 - 1070;*
  - *Listings of Professional Organizations, pgs. 1071 - 1073.*

- ***1001 Ways to Market Your Books*, by John Kremer: Chapter 2 - Planning** *- The Basis for Successful Marketing - What's to be included in a Marketing Plan, as well as, insights for you to follow.*

- ***The Fine Print of Self-Publishing – Fourth Edition, by Mark Levine***

6.2 Marketing Budget

In this section, describe how much money you are willing to spend to promote and publicize your book. You need to align your marketing goals with what you are willing / able to spend. If you do not have much money to spend, then you are going to have to rely on low cost to no cost marketing / promotional activities, such as:

- *Word-of-mouth*
- *Being a guest-speaker at local organizations*
- *Doing your own solicitations for book reviews, interviews, and media appearances*
- *Creating and distributing your own press releases*
- *Providing free copies of your book as door prizes, raffle prizes, or event giveaways*

Of course, if you have a larger marketing budget, you will have many more opportunities, such as:

- *Advertising via direct mail and / or purchasing email lists*
- *Setting up extensive author tours*
- *Advertising on TV and Radio stations*
- *Purchase large online marketing campaigns*
- *Purchase trade show booths*
- *Advertise in national and international markets*
- *Distributing other marketing promotional items*

6.3 Marketing Schedule
In this section, describe how much time you are willing to spend on promoting and publicizing your book. Make sure your timeline expands at least three years, and remember that marketing is an on-going process which will most likely require you to re-visit and update your Book Marketing Plan.

Before your book is complete:

- *Collect names and email addresses through social media*
- *Write press releases*
- *Write an author Bio*
- *Write a description of your book*
- *Create and distribute promotional items, like bookmarks*
- *Create a Blog and work towards getting a following*

First Year, after your book is published:

- *Distribute press releases*
- *Schedule book signings*
- *Solicit book reviews*
- *Direct sales campaigning (Book Fairs / Festivals, etc.)*

Second and Third Year, after your book is published:

- *Concentrate on your sales efforts and maintaining sales*
- *Continue your Internet marketing efforts*
- *Continue scheduling speaking engagements*
- *Expand your retail sales market*
- *Expand your advertising*

7. Proposed Promotional Fit
In this section, describe how your proposed book promotion fits in with major company objectives and ongoing research.

8. Other Author Comments on Marketing
In this section, state any other comments you have about your marketing efforts.

- *There are no hard and fast rules. Gather as much information as you can, try what you think you'll like and can afford, then see how it works.*
- *Two Key Concepts - Networking and putting yourself out there through Internet and in person.*
- *Try doing it yourself before paying someone else.*
- *Opportunities to promote and sell your books are all around you.*

CONCLUSION

Now that I have given you the major components of a BMP, and a template for making your own plan, this should give you a solid jump-start in getting your Book Marketing Plan created. Once you are done creating your BMP, your next step is to implement your BMP and continue to re-visit and update your BMP as new marketing strategies become available to you.

Happy Marketing.

- Mary D. Scott, PMP

About the Author

Mary Scott is a certified Project Management Professional (PMP), an Independent Verification and Validation / Quality Assurance Specialist for large complex mission critical information technology systems, an Author, and a Spiritual Healer. She lives in Southern California and is an active member of the High Desert Branch of the California Writers Club. She has promoted several "Meet the Authors" events to make known other published members of the branch. She has also participated in the construction of the branch web site pages of www.hdcwc.org and coordinated panels of writers to include publishing and marketing of their works.

Mary has written and self-published the book *Spirit Driven Events – Fascinating and Enlightening True Stories.* She is the software developer of the "*QAT SLC Success Tool Kit – The Key to Successful IT Projects*", which is based on the IEEE standards; and the "*QAT PM Tool Kit – The Key to Successful Project Management*", which is based on the PMI® PMBOK®Guide. She also developed courseware for the *QAT PM Academy*, which includes training courseware for PMI® *PMBOK Basics, PM Applied, PMP Test Prep*, and *IEEE Standards.* She is currently working on completing a technical series of books for the Information Technology Professional that she expects to publish in 2012.

Please visit: www.spiritdrivenevents.com

Reader's Note Page

www.ingramcontent.com/pod-product-compliance
Lightning Source LLC
Chambersburg PA
CBHW081228170526
45165CB00009B/3002